I am grateful to God for everything! And I believe that the meaning of life is to make sense of other lives. You are the meaning of my life.

Daniel Rosa de Mattos

2024

This Book Belongs to:

○─────────────────────────────────○

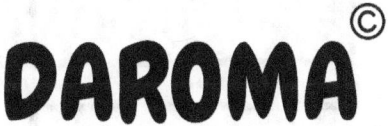

Test Color Page

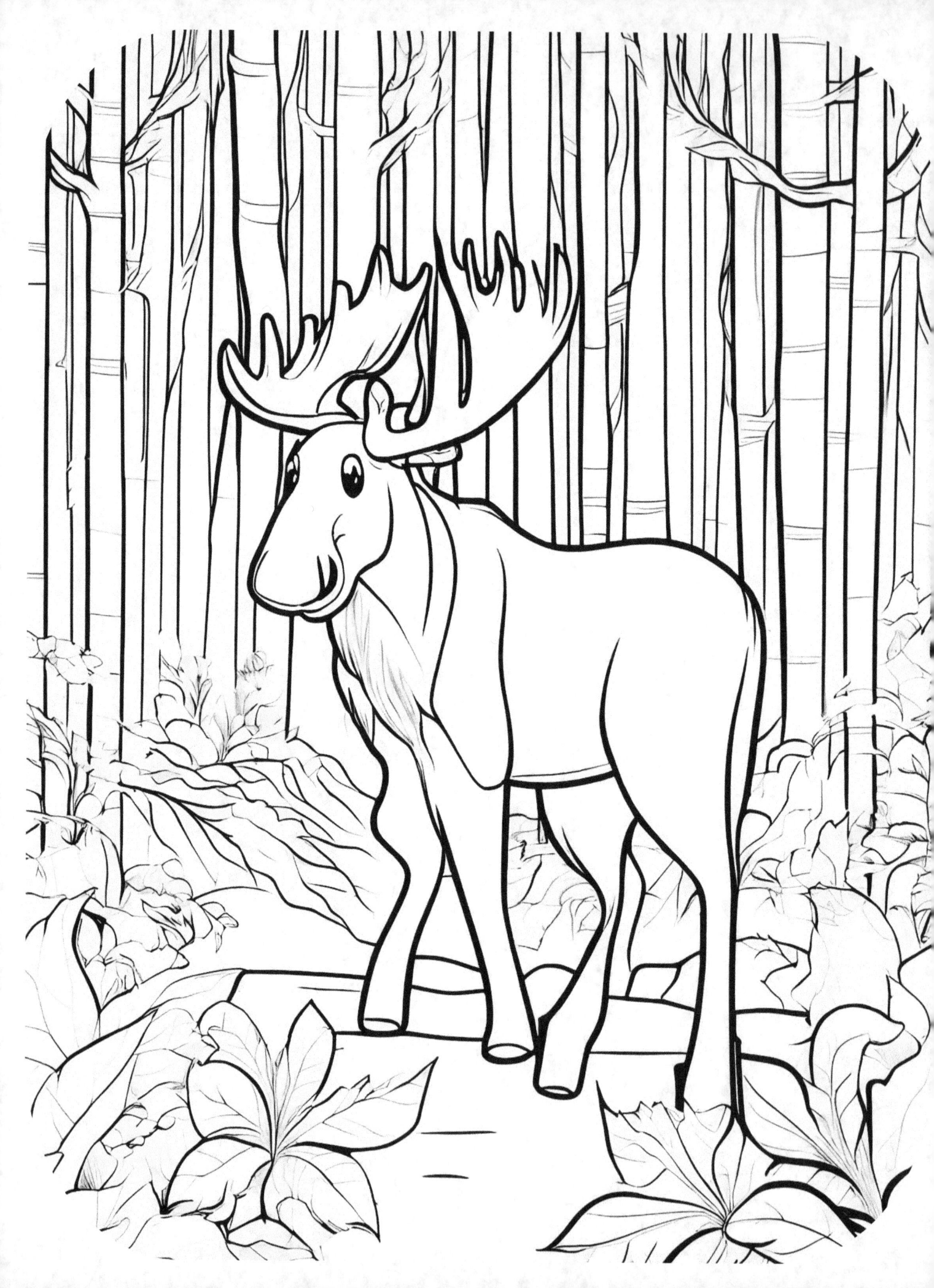

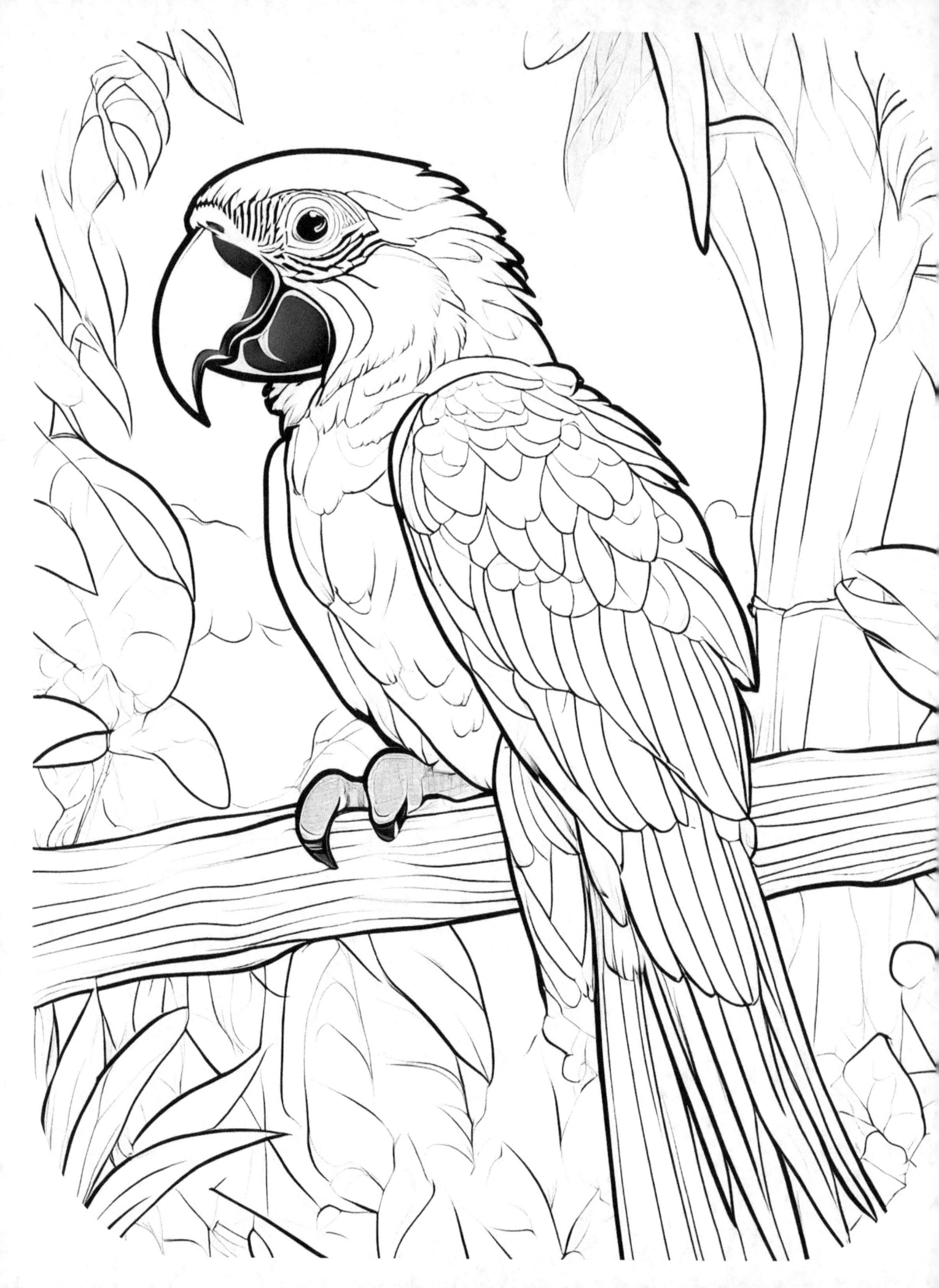

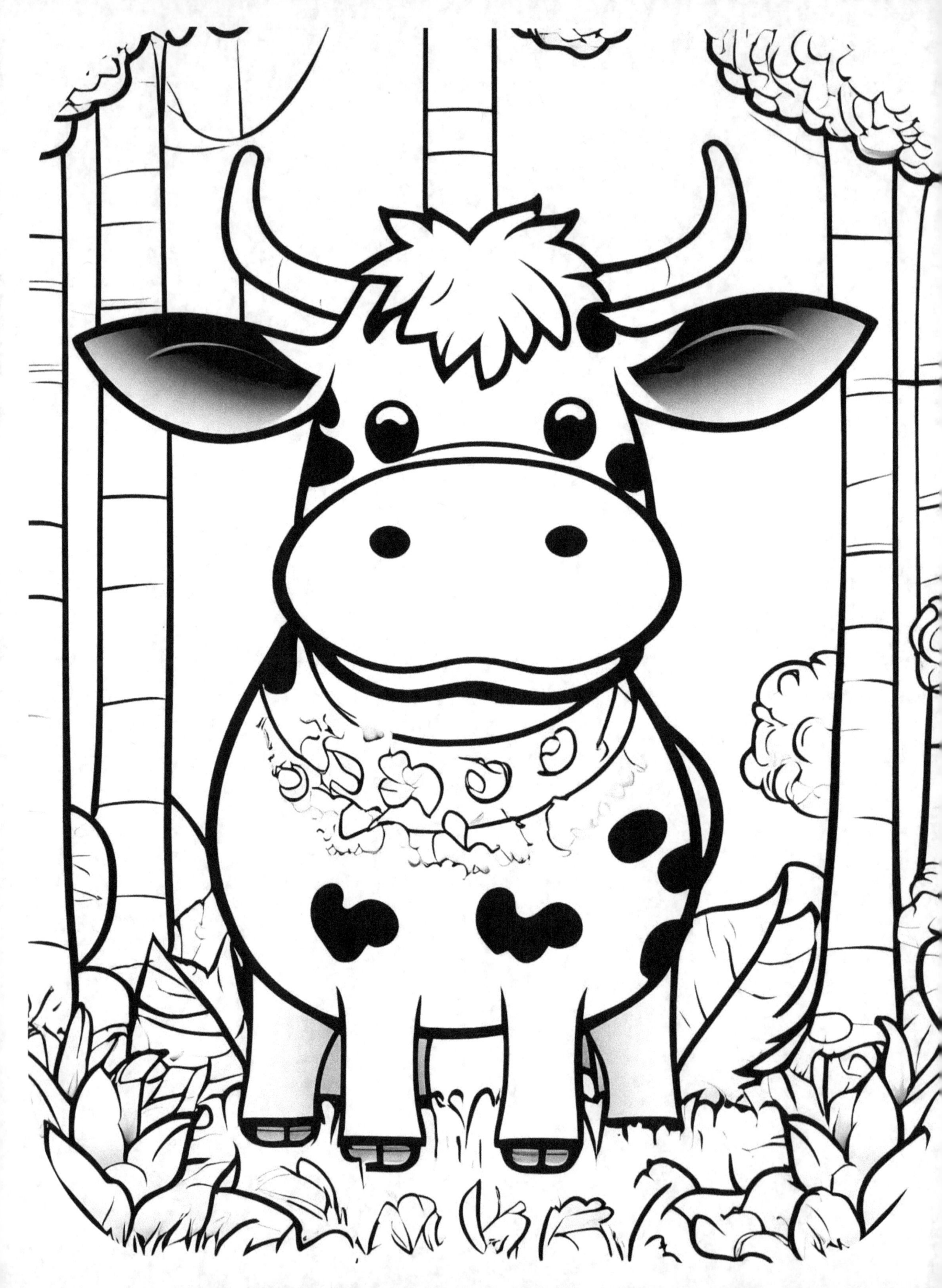

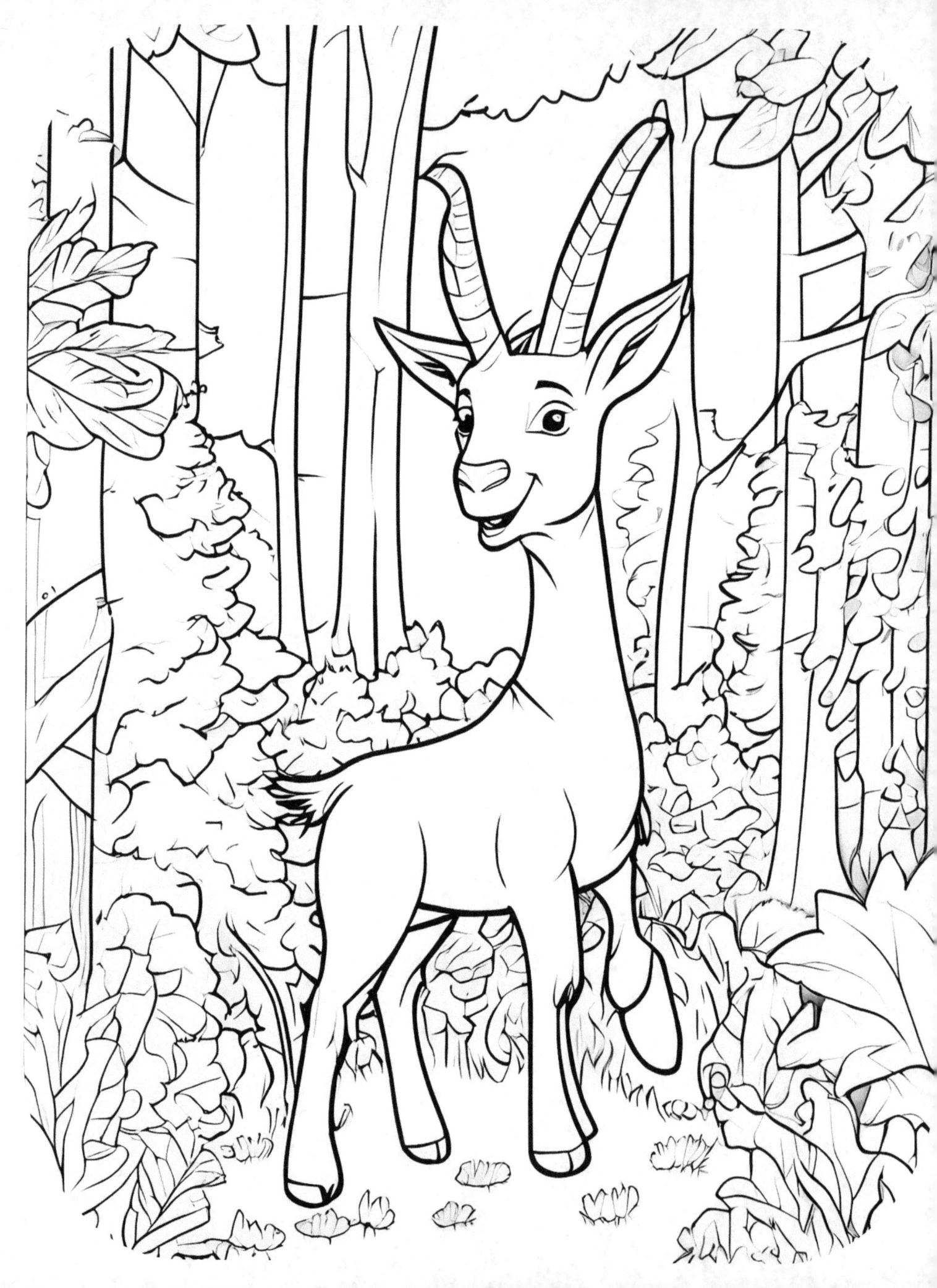

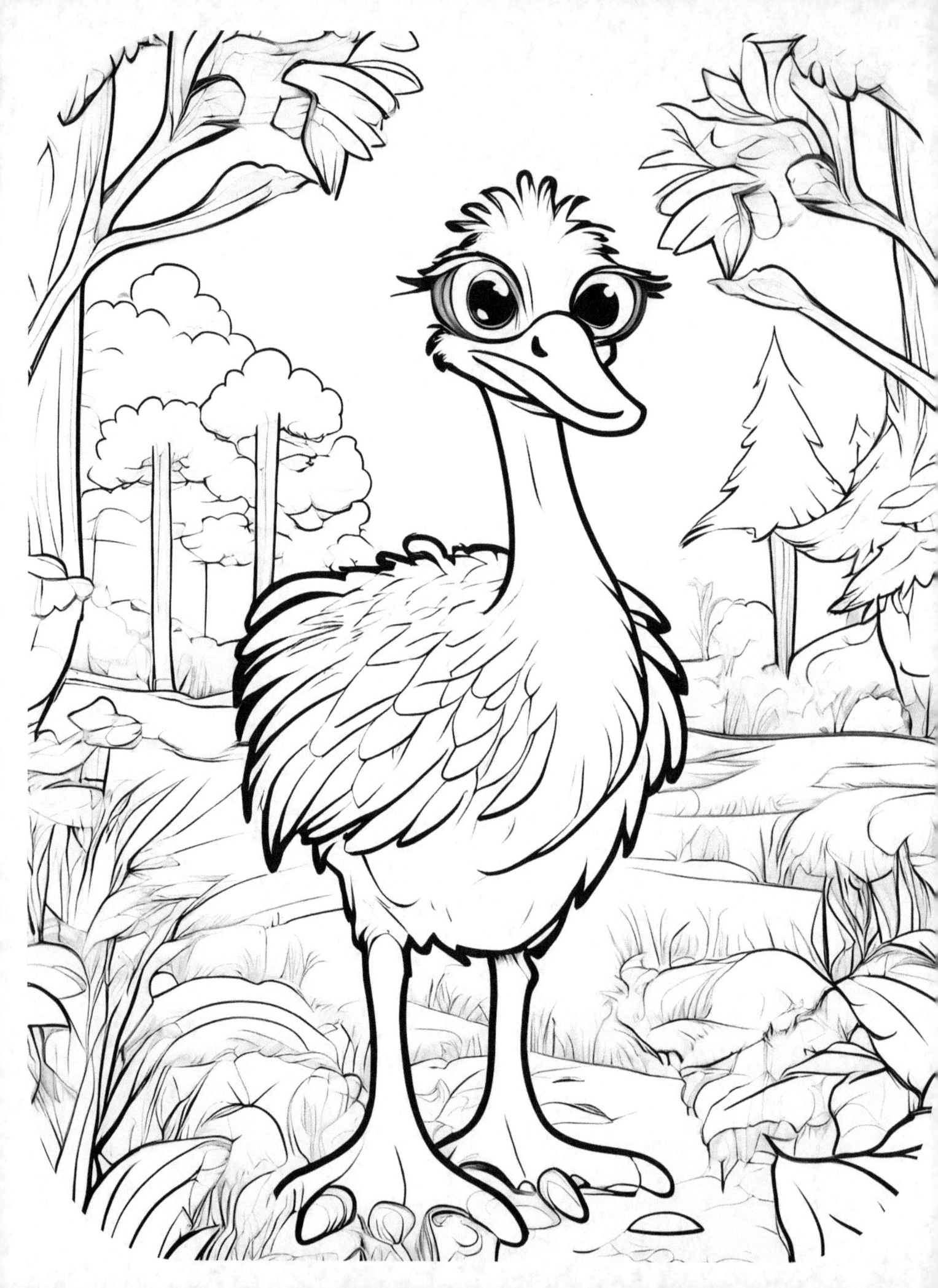

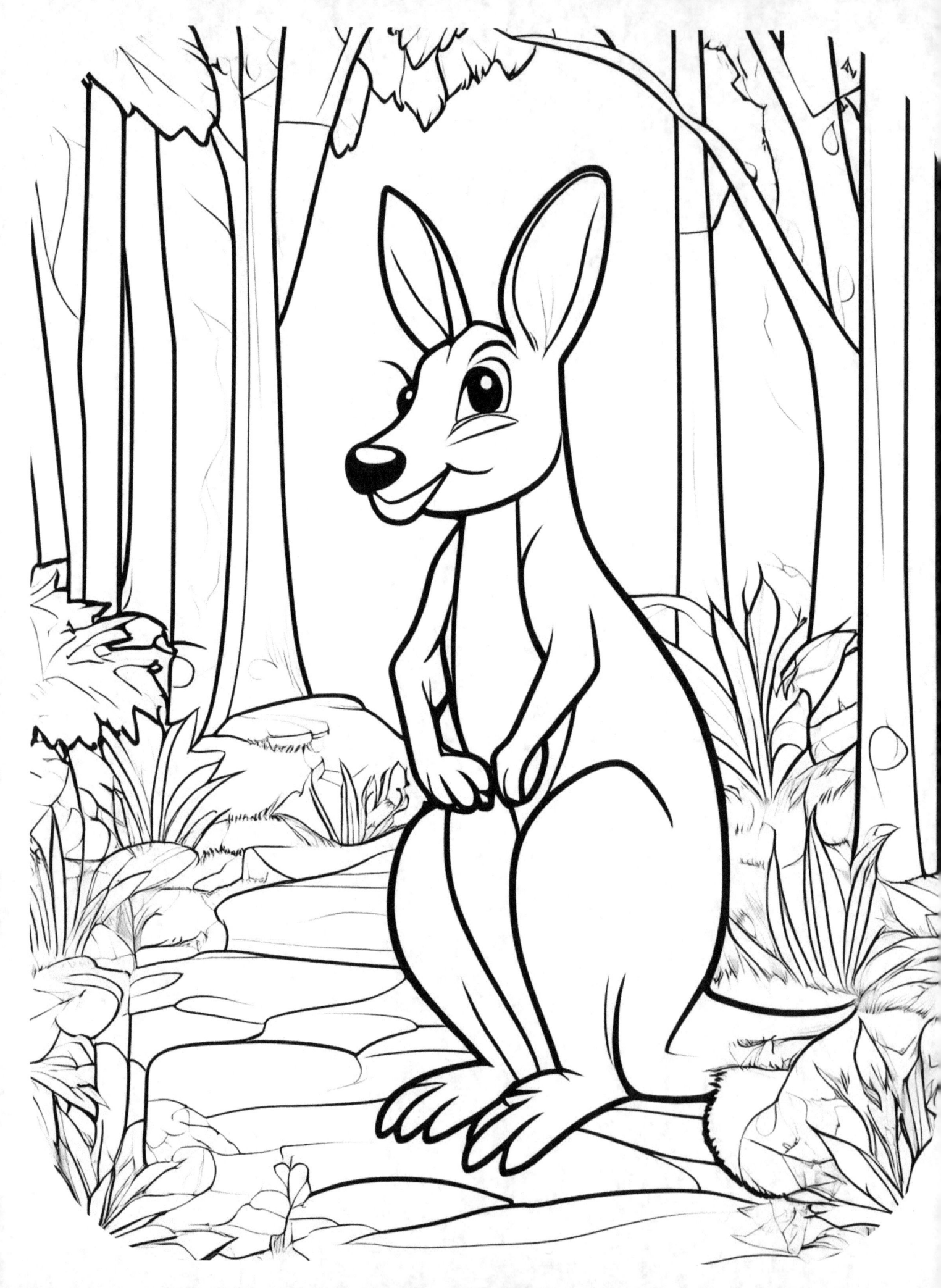

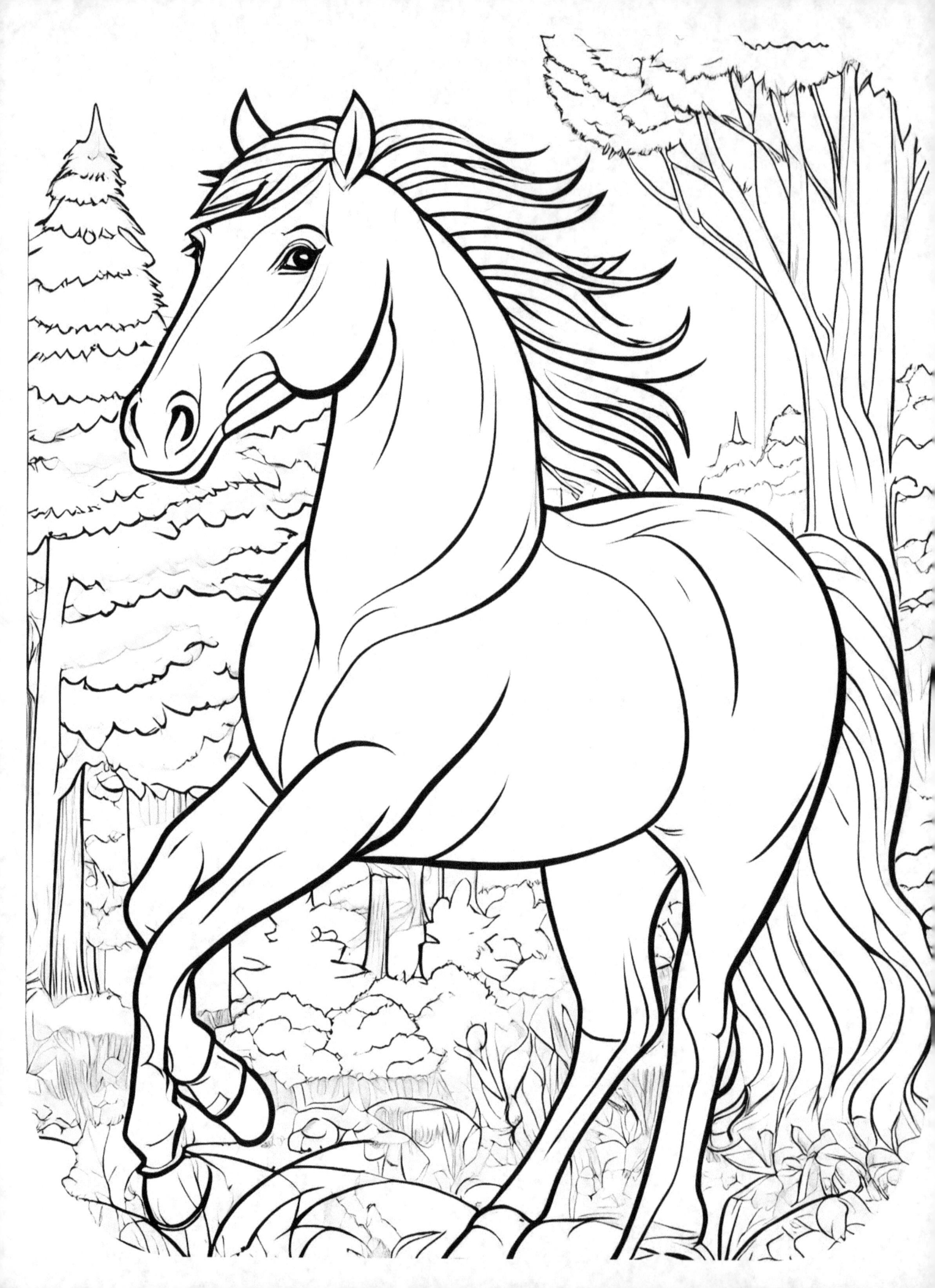

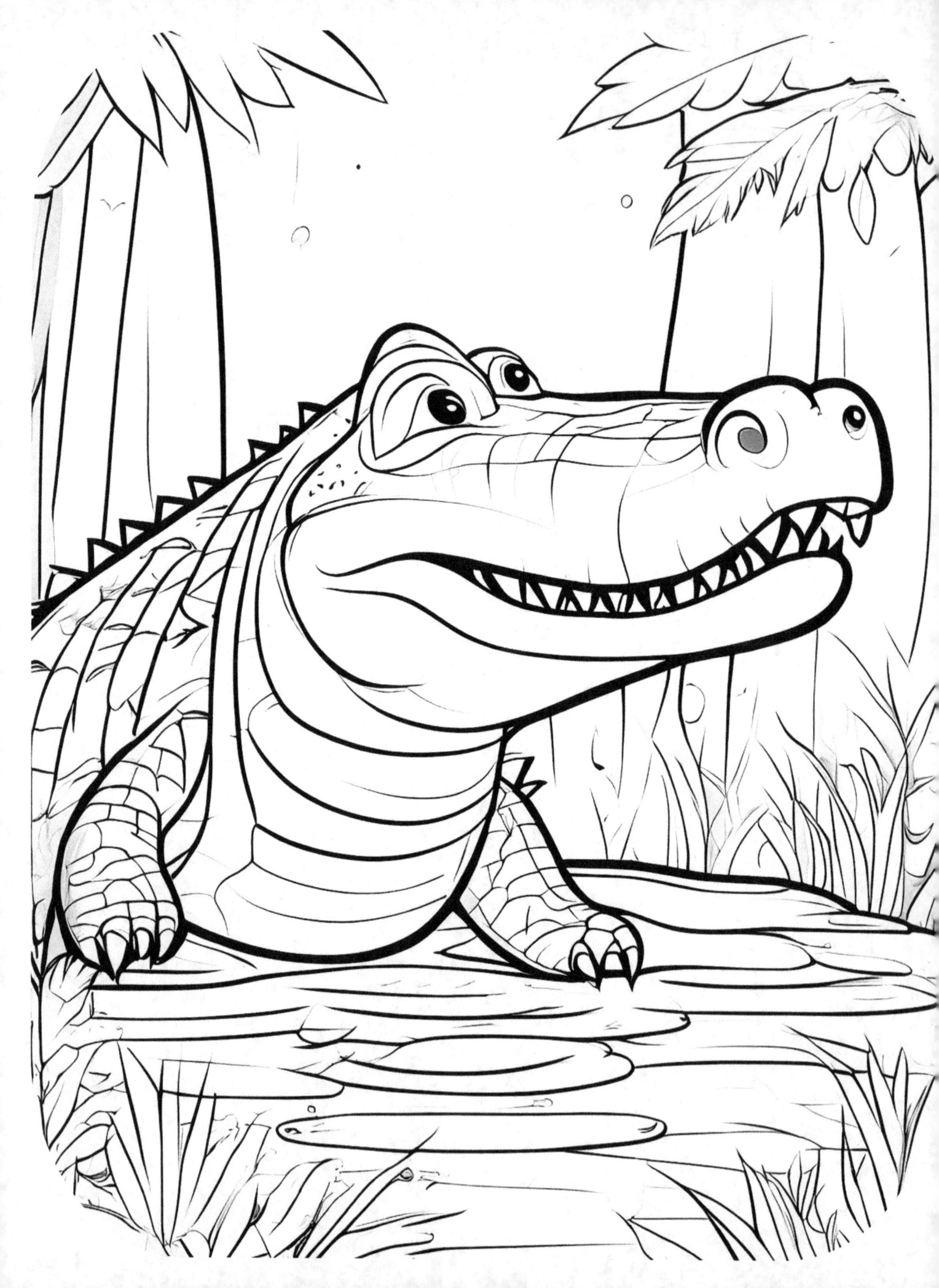

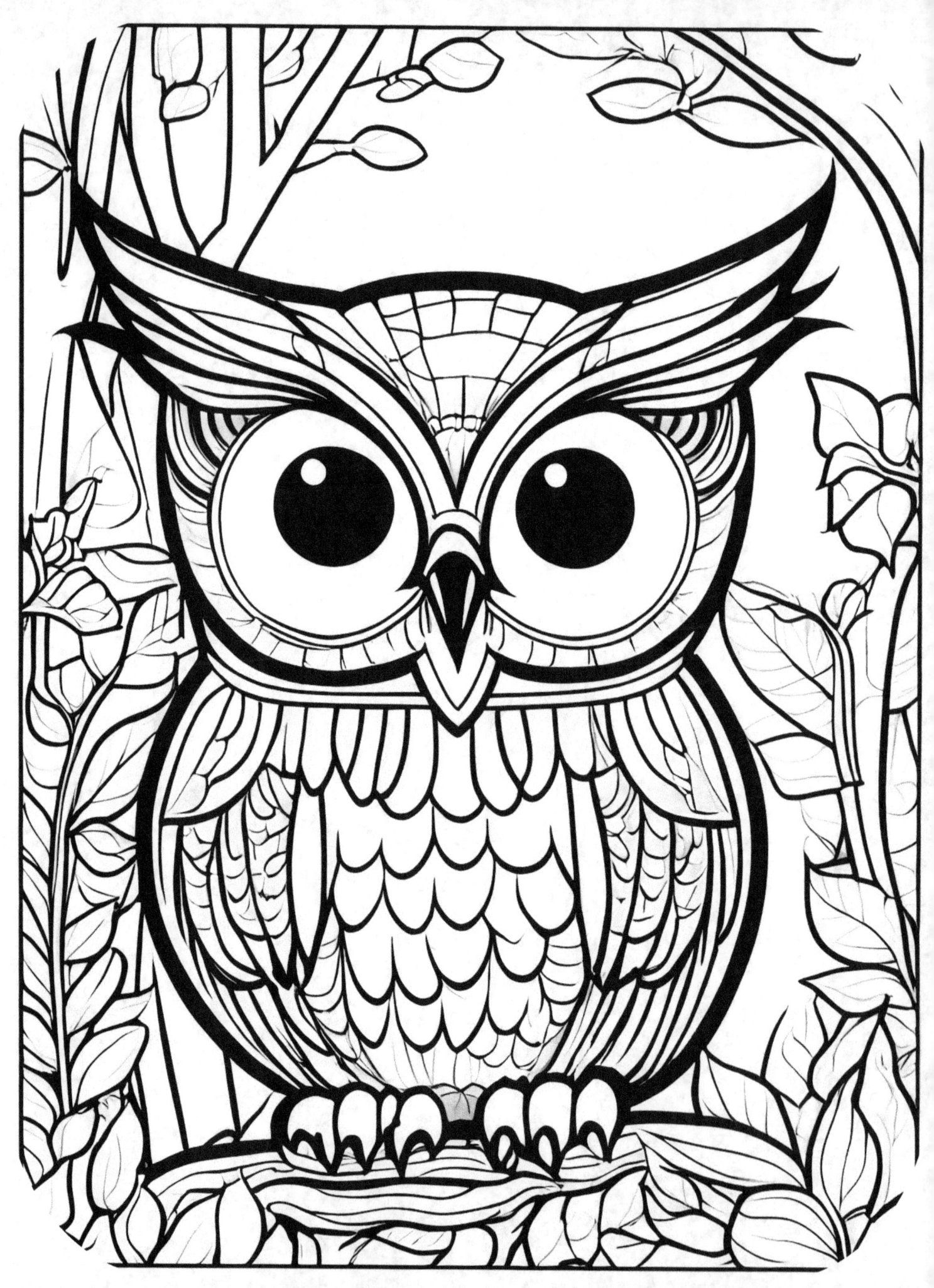

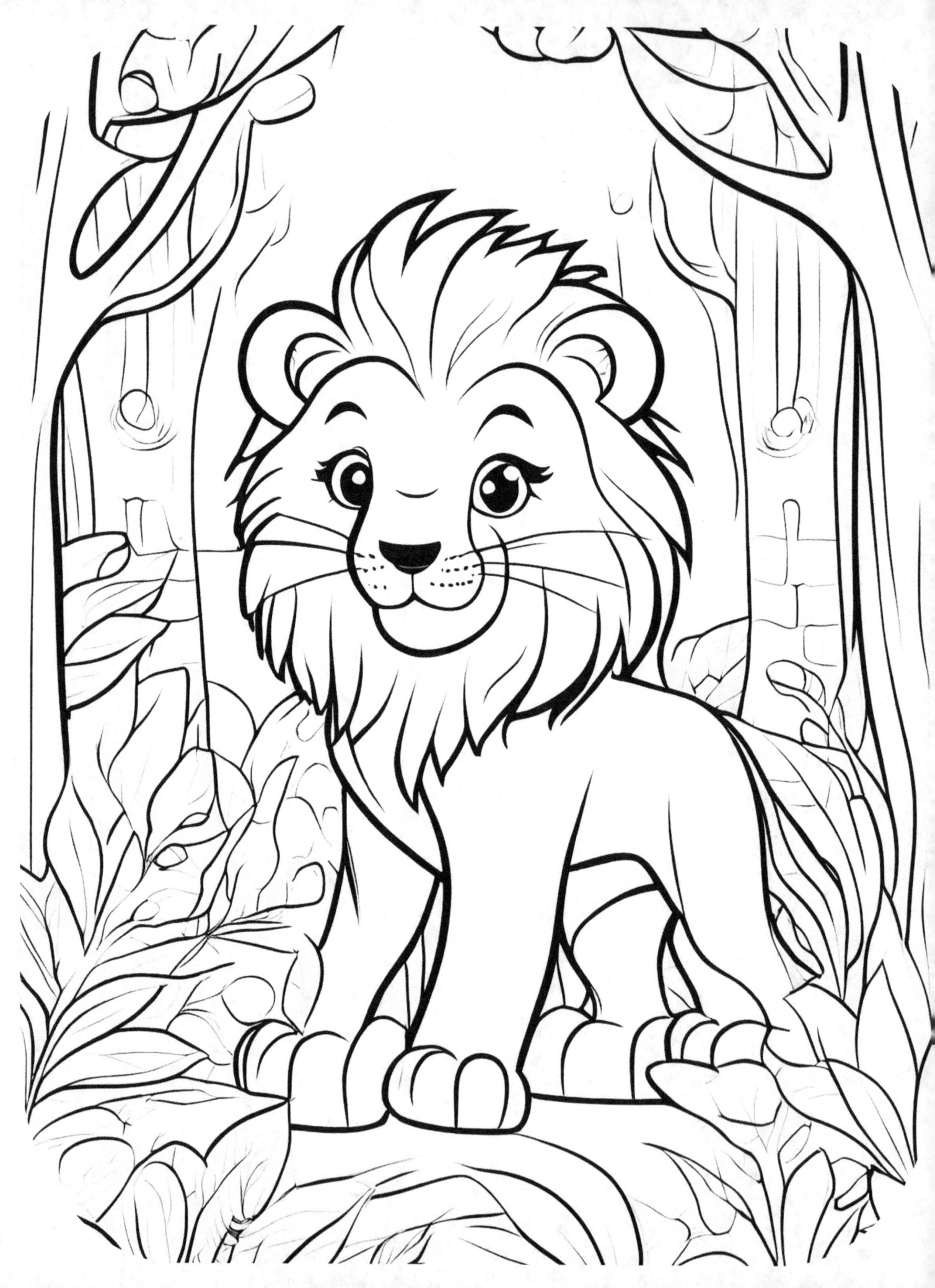

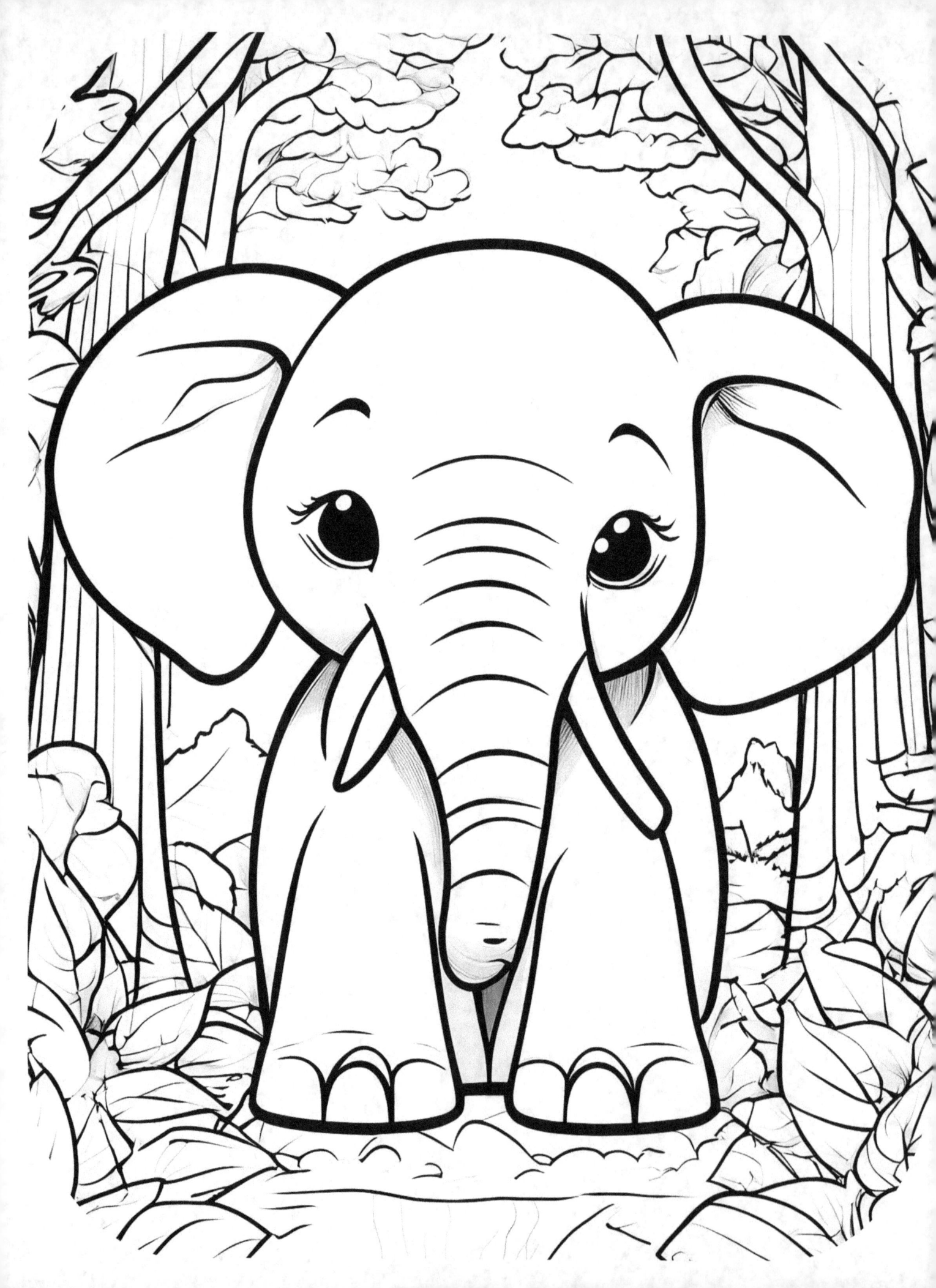

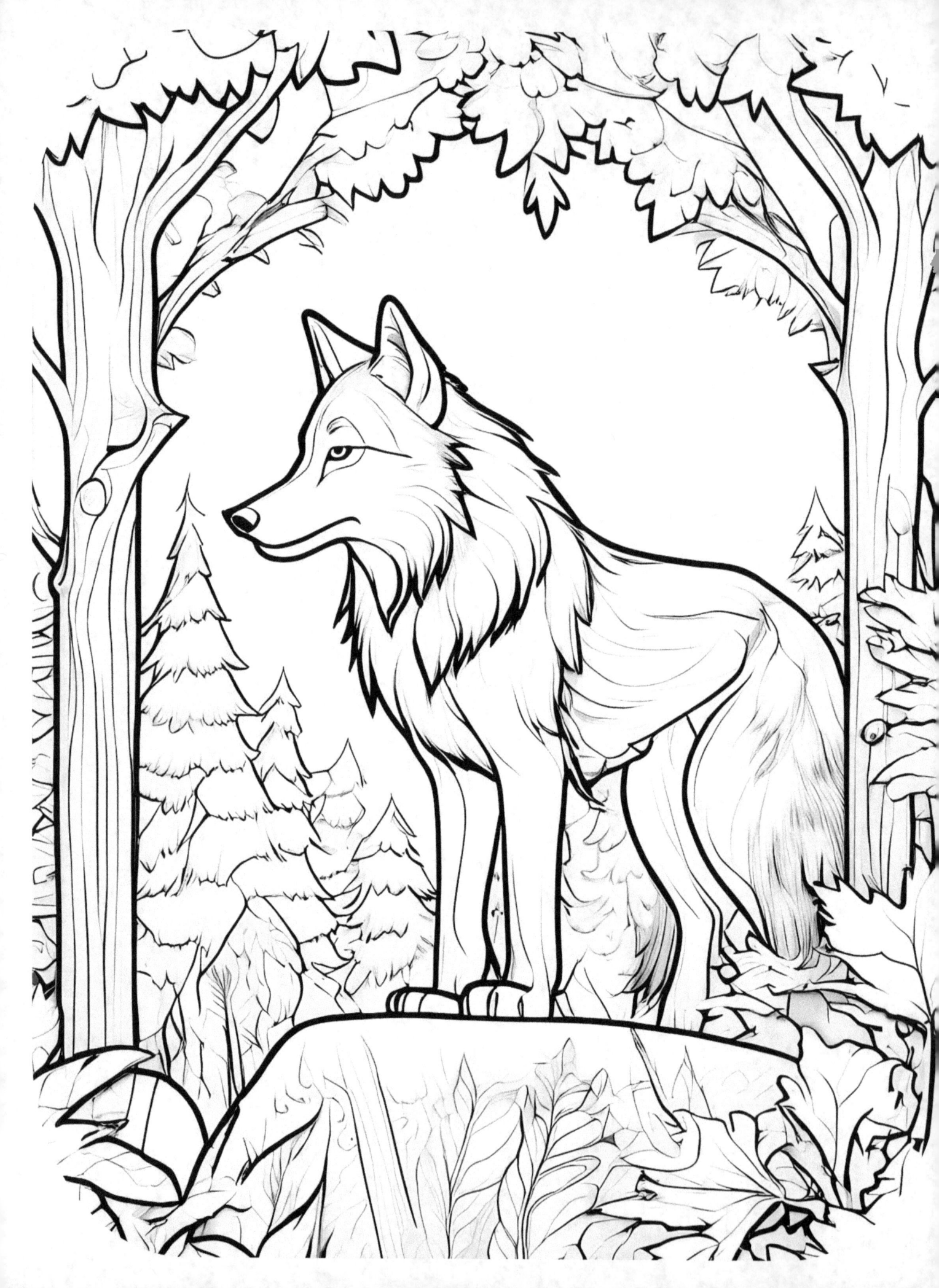

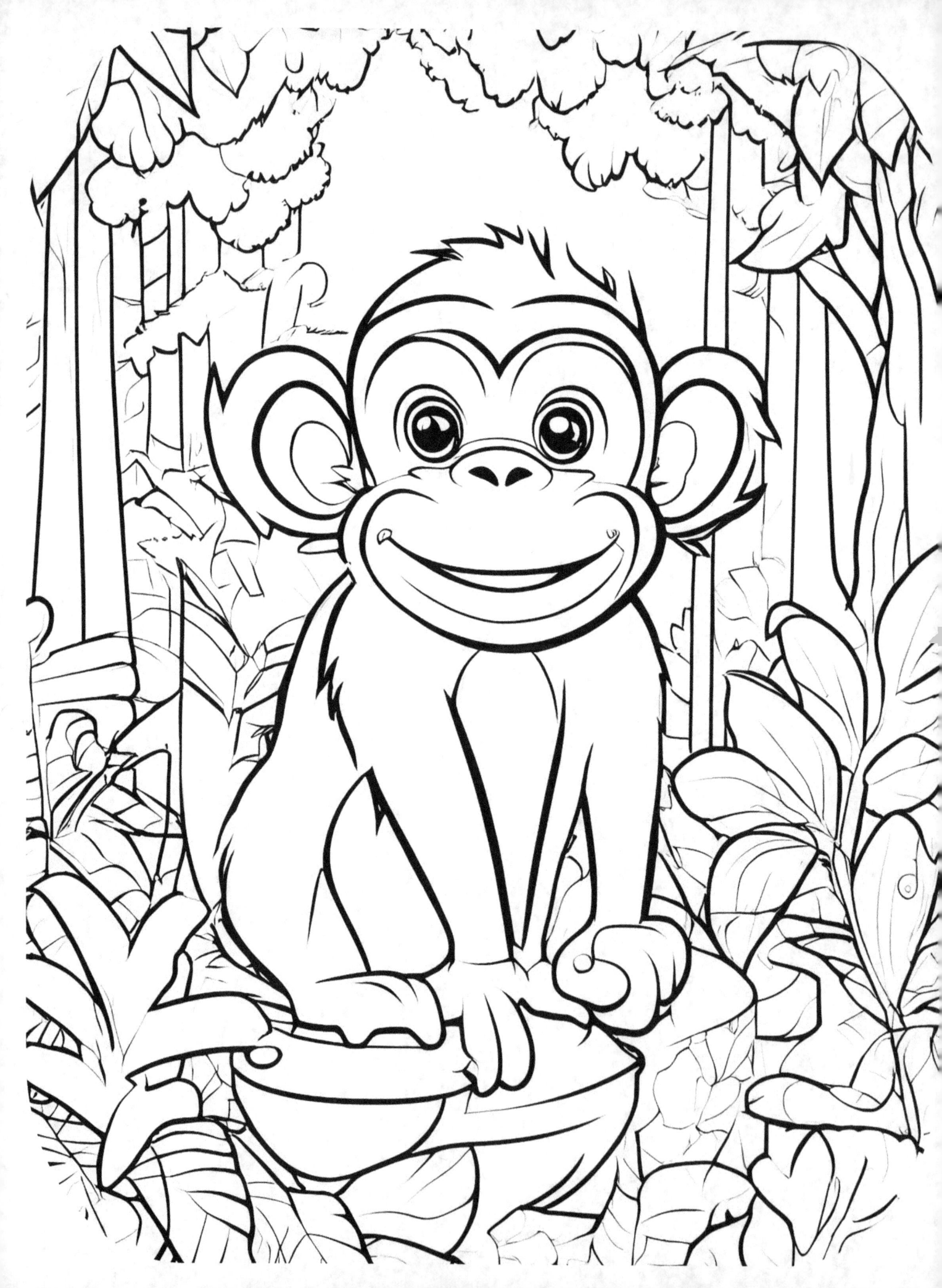

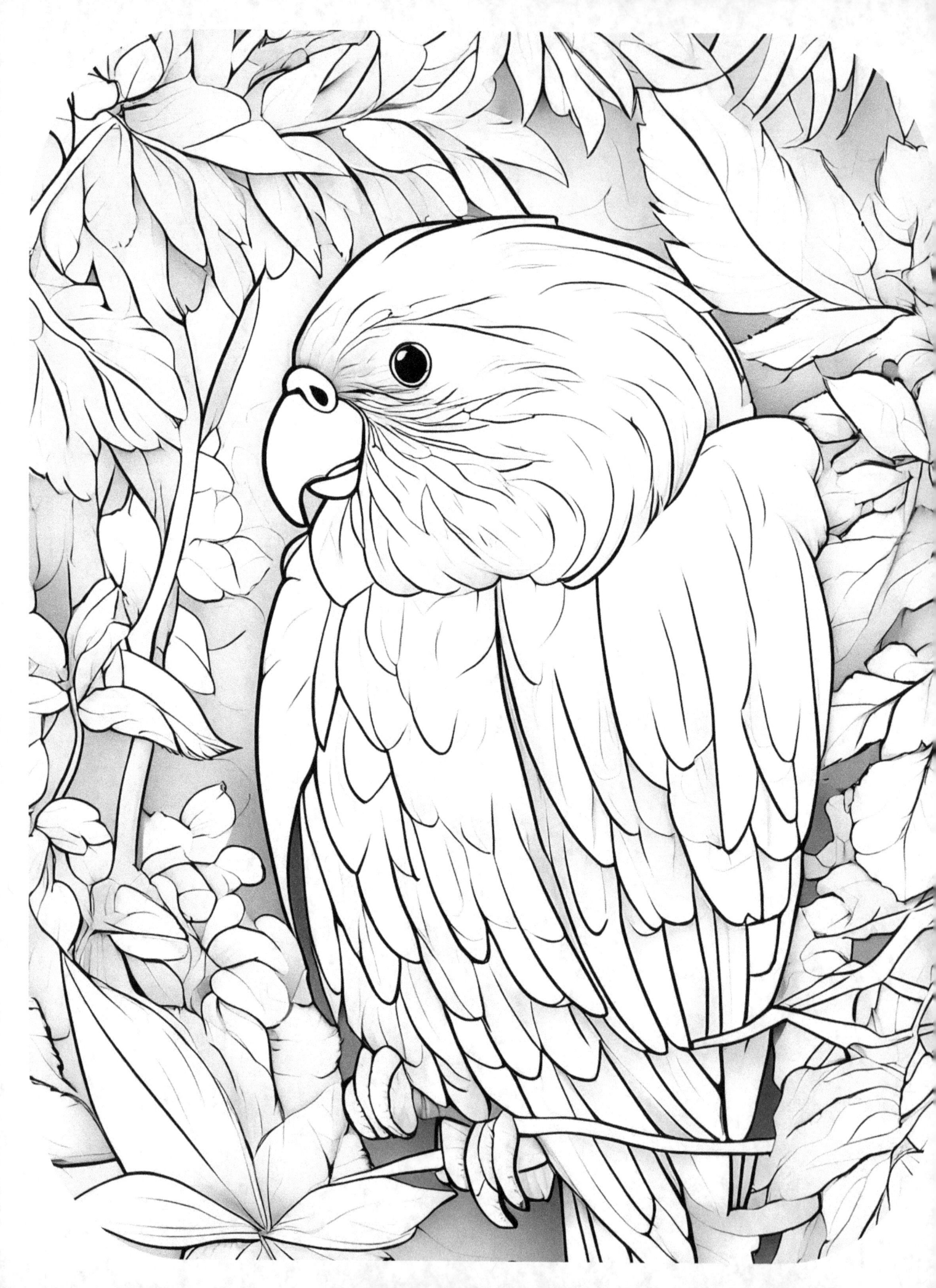

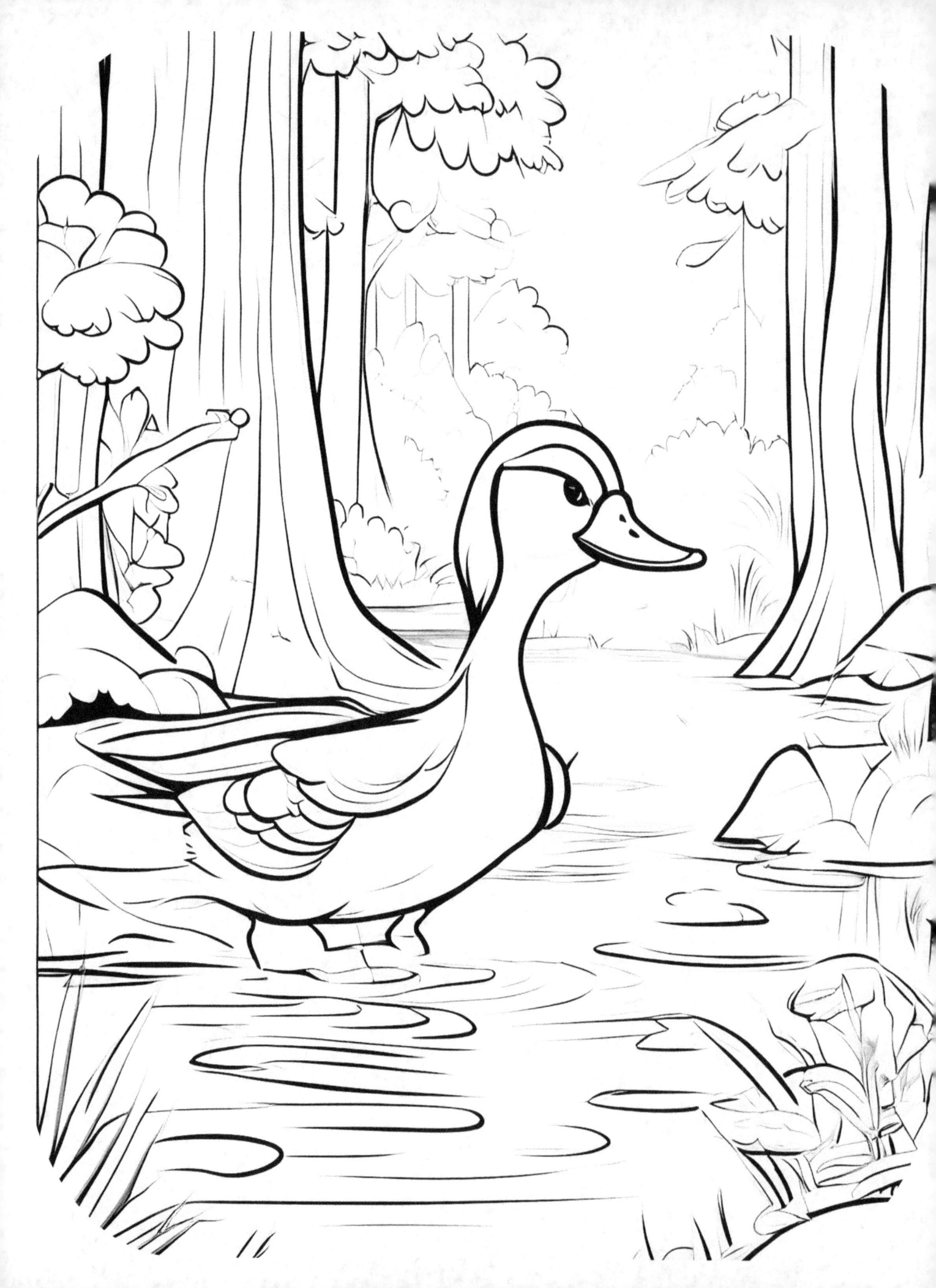

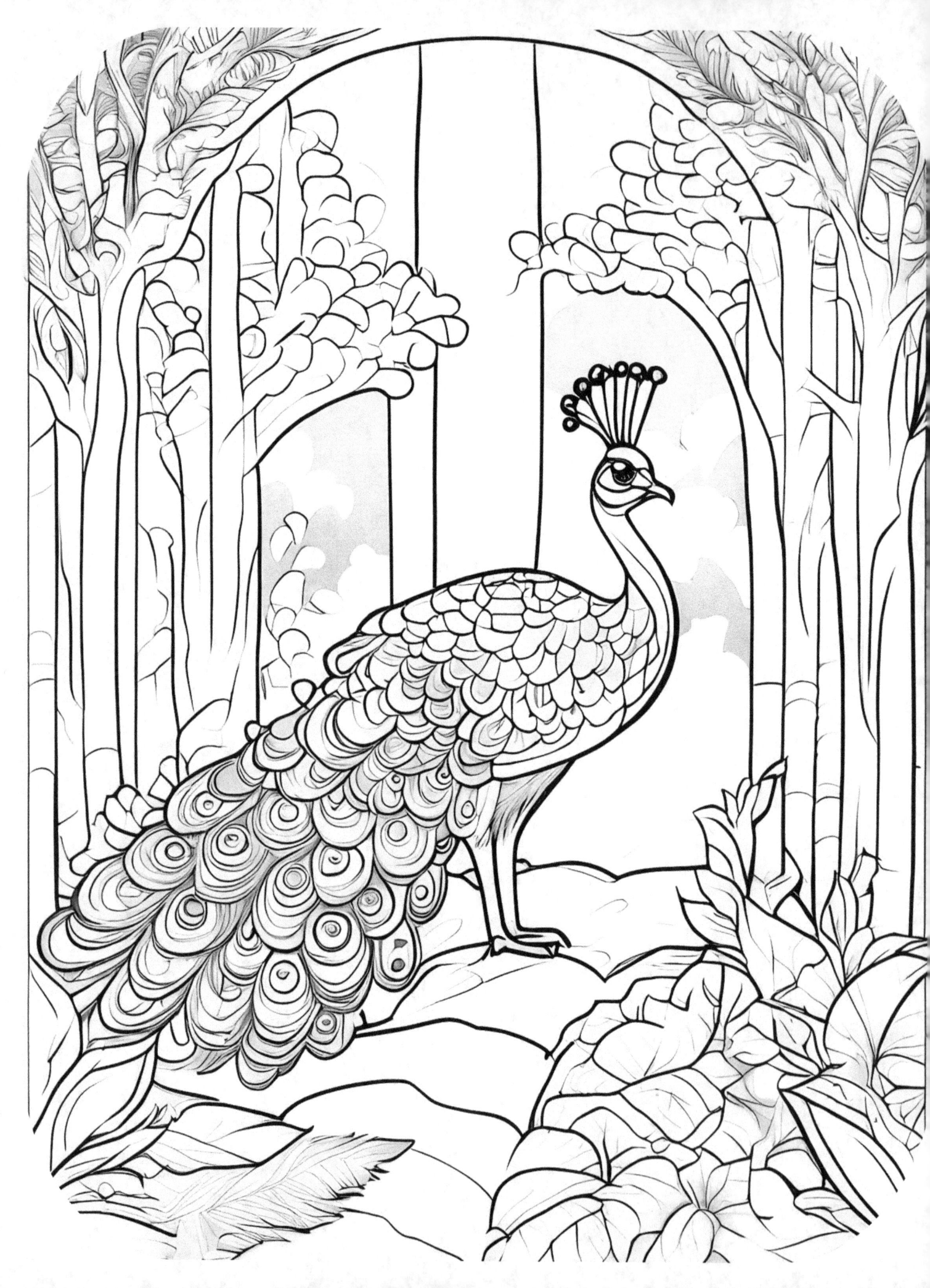

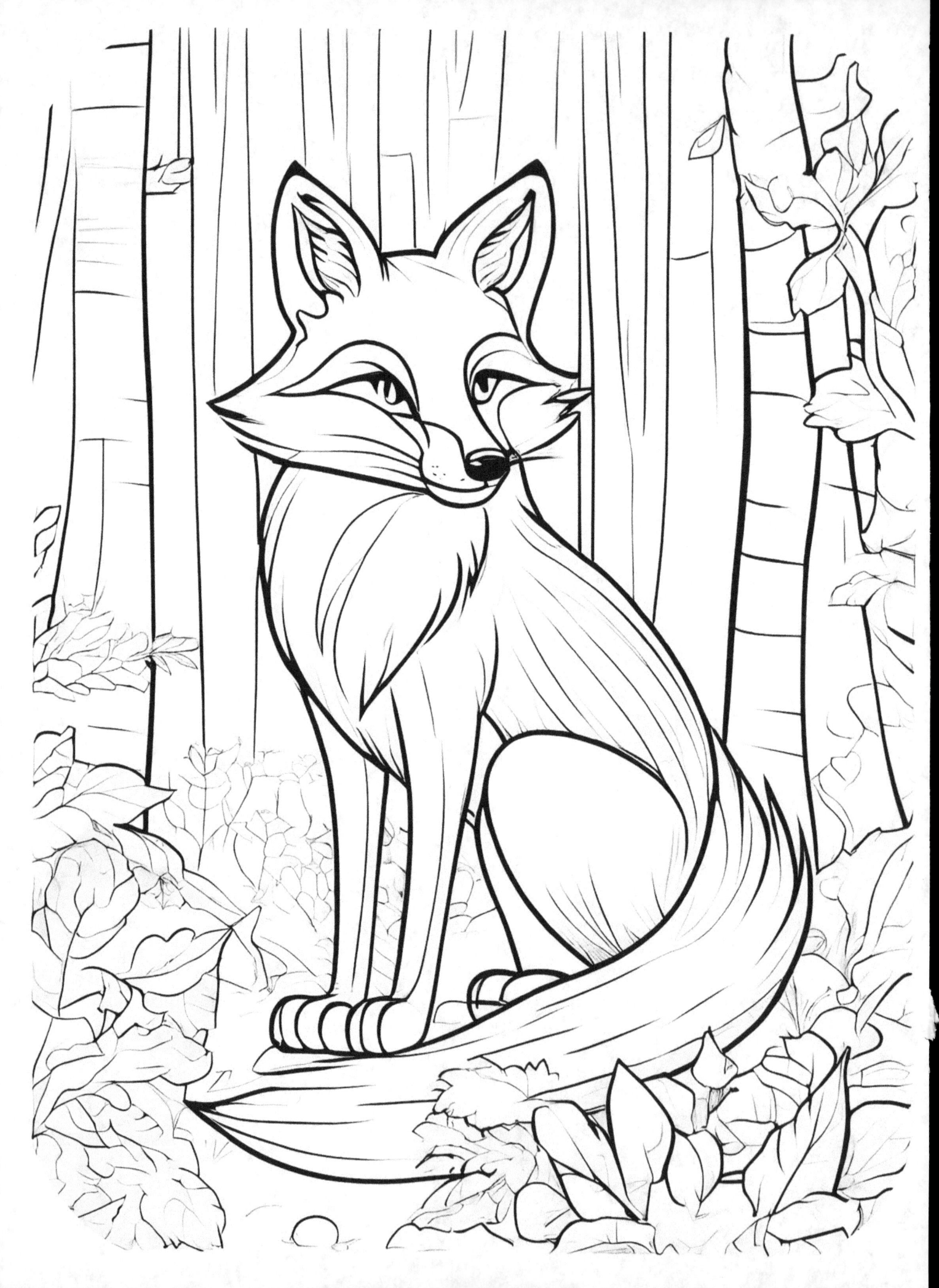

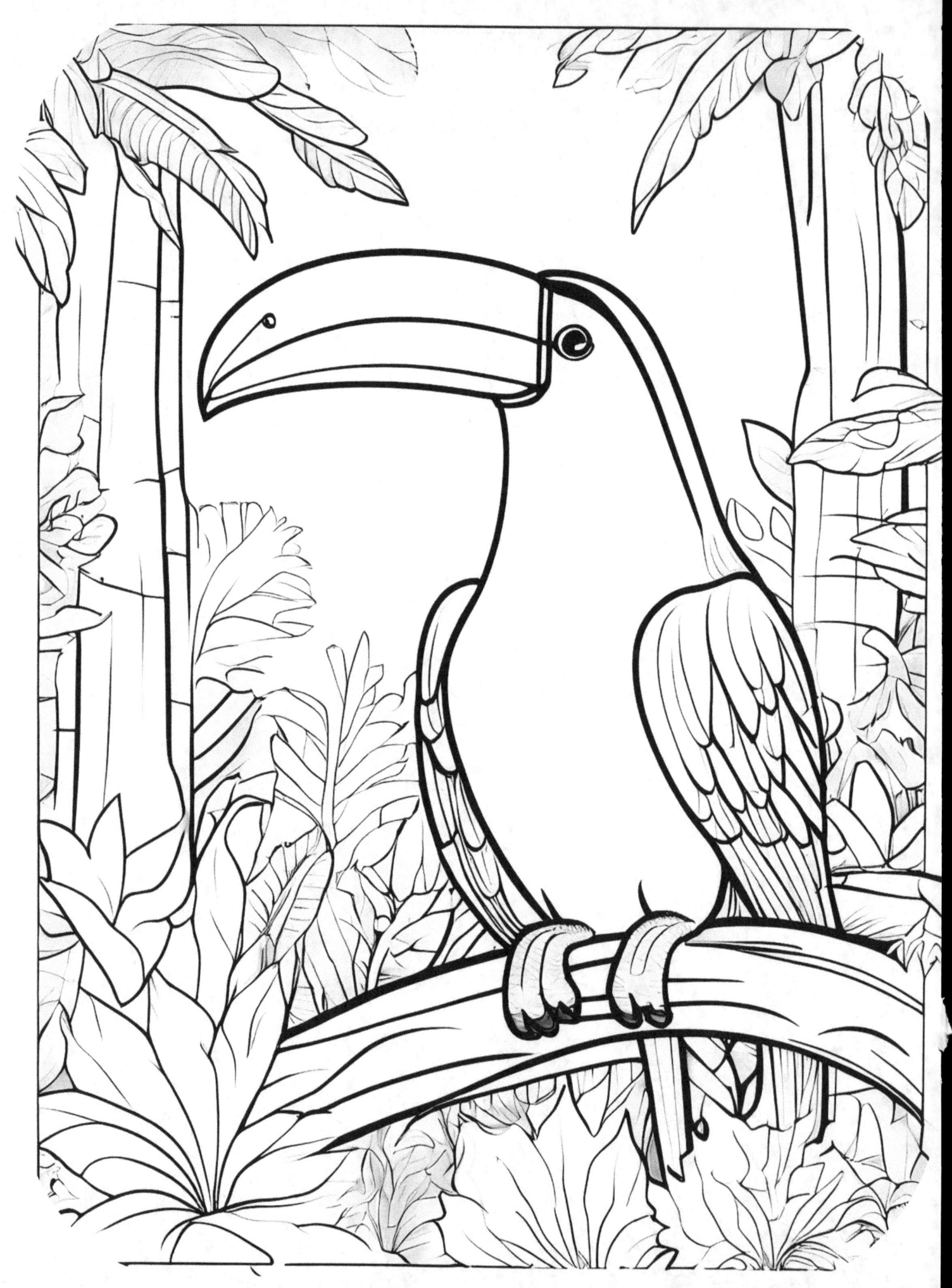

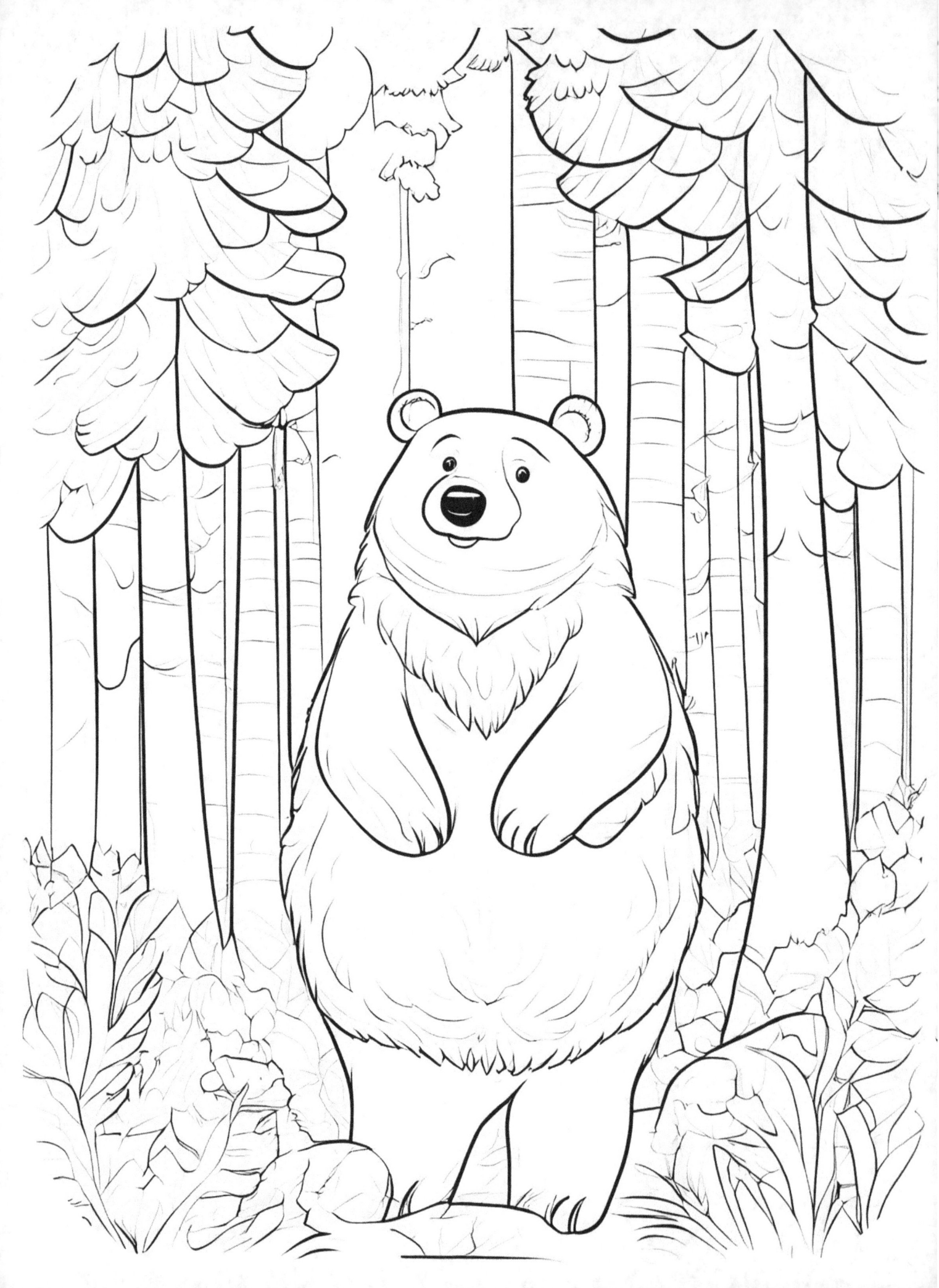

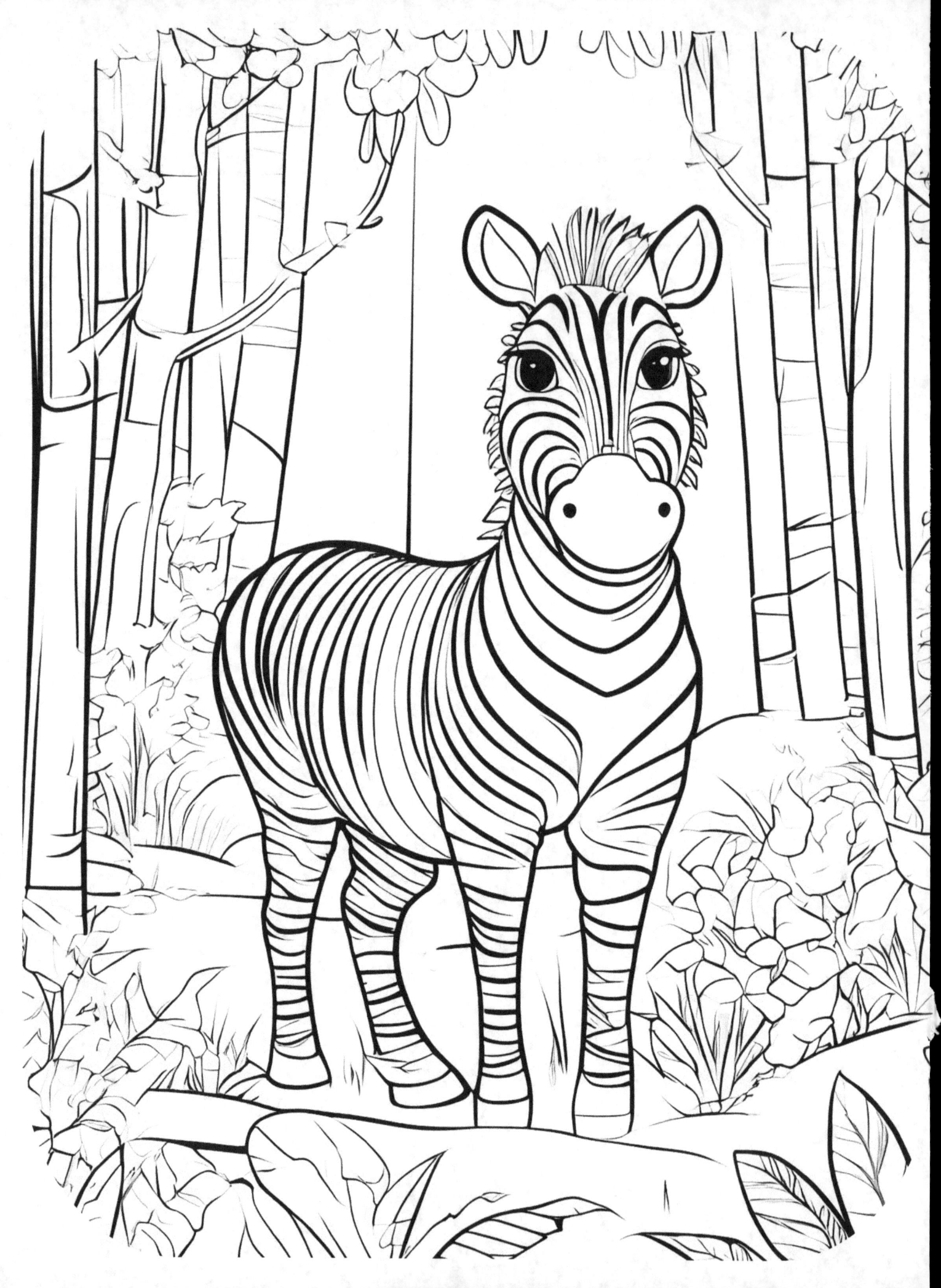

www.ingramcontent.com/pod-product-compliance
Lightning Source LLC
Chambersburg PA
CBHW081003290526
45795CB00009B/3061